"Can't this singing be / one brief note that / (some / net // and flings it back to God?" wonders Elizabeth Pinborougn in this, her debut collection—and indeed, *The Brain's Lectionary* gazes fearlessly at any number of hard questions. About the body's betrayals. About the seeming indifference of God. And, fundamentally, about the unreliability of language itself. No lexicon will suffice to account for the serial mortifications of human experience, much less when the brain, our word-organ, has suffered a dis-ordering, de-*selving* shock. Pinborough attends to these hard questions with clear-eyed courage and remarkable compassion, offering up this new psalter on "new matter" that combines words, images, and silences to make legible the whole person, seen and unseen.

—Kimberly Johnson
author of *Uncommon Prayer*

Elizabeth Pinborough's debut hybrid poetry collection is immersive in its exploration of brain injury. She powerfully transcribes the embodied experience of a healing brain through remarkable formal inventiveness. Text breaks down. Language disintegrates into white space as words gape apart. Dashes convey neurons firing and rewiring in the gaps. Lines of poems mimic the peaks and valleys of brainwaves. As if that weren't enough, Pinborough intersperses her exquisite linocuts throughout—a pomegranate, an arrangement of diatoms—underscoring in this visual medium the text's motifs. Because Pinborough does the difficult labor of rendering visible a disability that is frequently invisible, this book will deepen readers' awareness and sensitivity, and will increase appreciation for that wondrously complex three-pound organ we too often take for granted.

—Dayna Patterson
author of *If Mother Braids a Waterfall*

Elizabeth Pinborough has done something remarkable with these poems, which are so beautifully creative that I'm awestruck. For many years I've thought of her as one of the finest poets writing today, and his collection confirms that in my mind. What is so transformative about these poems, and the affecting accompanying illustrations, is that she is working through a devastating traumatic brain injury that fractured her neuronal self. As a survivor of brain trauma, I am staggered by what she has overcome to create this book. She mixes science, art, and religious thought with a facility that is breathtaking. She transmutes her injury into a profound work of artistry and expression. These are powerful and gorgeously wrought poems, which somehow emerge from among the darkest places a human can go. She reaches down into the depth of her being and creates something extraordinary. We are so lucky to journey with her in reconnecting a fractured self with healing poetry of such grace and beauty. This collection is essential. It is poetry about redeeming trauma at the very core of what it means to be a person. Do not miss this unforgettable and unique contribution to the world.

—Steven L. Peck
author of *The Tragedy of King Leere,*
Goatherd of the La Sals

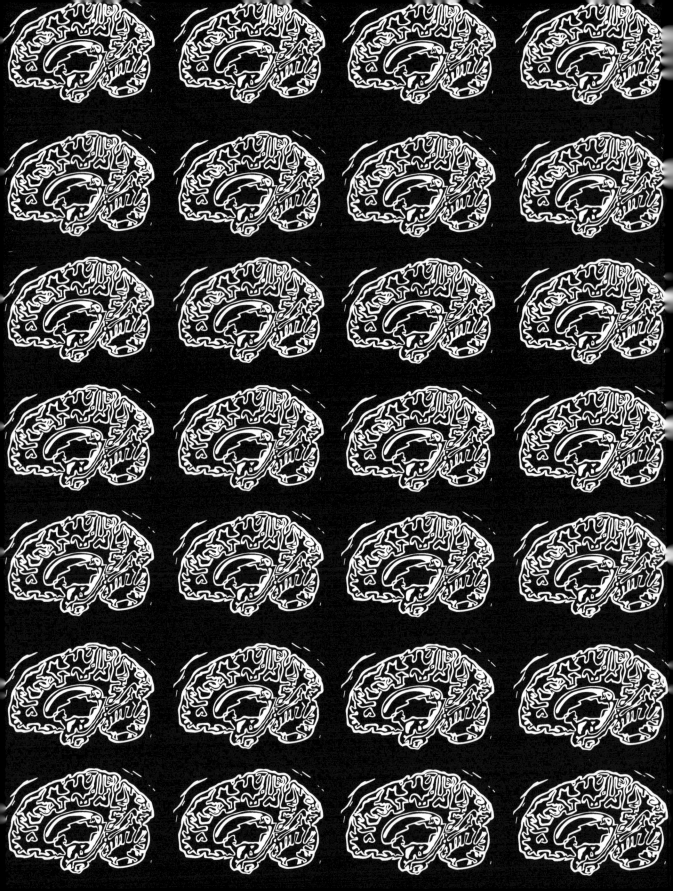

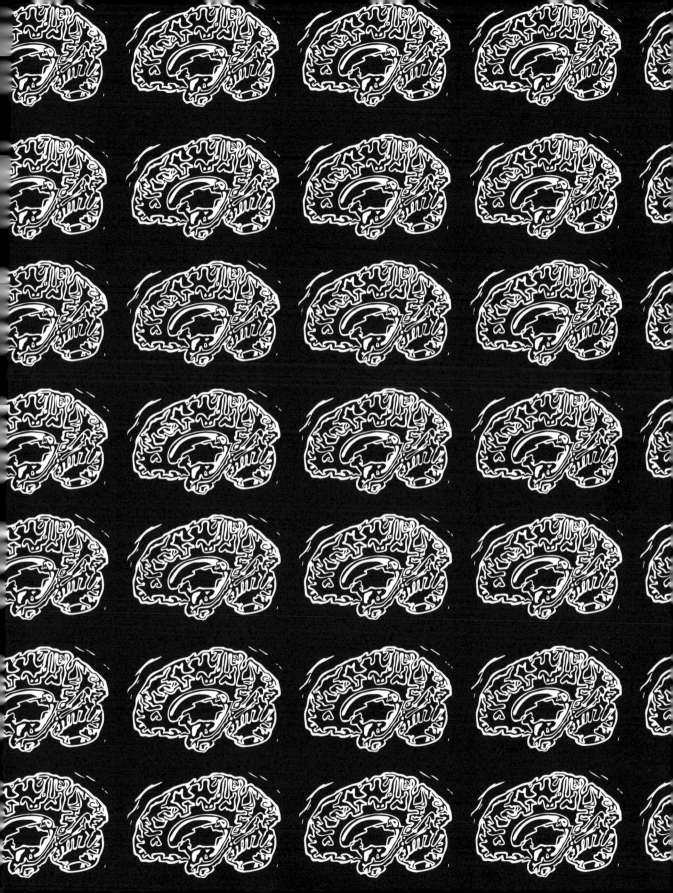

The Brain's Lectionary

Elizabeth Pinborough

By Common Consent Press is a non-profit publisher dedicated to producing affordable, high-quality books that help define and shape the Latter-day Saint experience. BCC Press publishes books that address all aspects of Mormon life. Our mission includes finding manuscripts that will contribute to the lives of thoughtful Latter-day Saints, mentoring authors and nurturing projects to completion, and distributing important books to the Mormon audience at the lowest possible cost.

The Brain's Lectionary

Psalms and Observations

Elizabeth Pinborough

For information contact
By Common Consent Press
4900 Penrose Dr.
Newburgh, IN 47630

Cover design: D Christian Harrison
Book design: Andrew Heiss

www.bccpress.org
ISBN-13: 978-1-948218-47-4

10 9 8 7 6 5 4 3 2 1

For Jan, Tom, and Christiana, with my love

For all who seek to rebuild their very selves

Hit a wall with your head.
—Yoko Ono, 1962

Nothing therefore can separate us from the love of God.
—Joseph Smith, 1839

Contents

. . . Oceans . . .

{tiny} Lights

Healing the Brain>>>

| Poems to God |

Introduction

The Brain's Lectionary is a book of hours. The psalms I wrote from the depths can be a series of readings for you in your darkest times. The occasion for this book was a traumatic brain injury I experienced in 2015. In verse and illustration, I tell of my voyage through the storm, my perilous near-drownings, and my fumblings for an astrolabe to guide me back to myself and back to God. The chaos of living with an injured brain is much like surviving a constant barrage of invisible electric shocks. I seek to make a few of the injuries that TBI survivors experience visible on paper and transform them into tiny nodes of light and hope.

Shape poems serve as strange devotions for inexpressibly hard times. Psalms lend a language of prayer when words to God won't come. Linocuts serve as icons on which readers may meditate. Like inscrutable X-rays or MRIs, they are black and white, revealing little about the fullness of their contours or the imagined depths of their disrepair. As with any injury invisible to the untrained eye, one image or one frame is never the final story. So much more knowledge awaits us as we explore.

Healing from major injury, illness, or crisis requires almost religious devotion and sometimes brings with it stifling isolation. Time is hardly regular when home is your hospital. The sacred may have lost its lustre. The holy lesson for any given day may be completely illegible, your usual patterns of worship disrupted. When there is no discernible progress on the pilgrim's path, God may feel inaccessible eons away. Many walking wounded carry burdens that need the comfort of a friend who has been there. I hope this book may be that friend.

In an injured brain, religious hope can be discomfiting rather than soothing. To continue to heal, I have needed to make and remake the shattered meanings of my life thousands of times. When the most precious meanings of your life have been ripped away, the suggestion that there is ultimate meaning, or purpose in pain, offers little hope. Meaning cannot make some experiences bearable. The failure of language is one of the final frontiers of human suffering. How can we rest in God when the thought of God isn't restful, when God does not intervene to cease chronic pain?

I am not sure I have the answers. I attempt to muster some here by looking into the depths of the sea and the convolutions of my brain. I create new connections, and I invite you to do the same. Now with a brain more healed, I feel meaning and purpose again. But to bypass the destruction of my *self* that I endured in the searing heat of my own skull was not possible. The journey was interior and forward at a snail's pace. Not over, not around. Through.

Writing this book is an act of literary, linguistic, artistic, and theological reconstitution. Typographic experimentation and expressiveness are key. Mimicking the way eighty billion individual neurons in the brain communicate across synapses to become functional networks, I organize chaotic dots, symbols, and spaces into coherent clusters. I hope they form a whole, with gaps that speak, mean, and heal in new ways. I am putting my self back together.

May *The Brain's Lectionary* be a faithful companion for anyone in extremity—those living with the long-term consequences of brain injury, chronic health concerns, or any trauma that shatters the body and the relationship with self. For those who are living with physical, mental, psychological, and spiritual suffering, I hope you will find the comfort of shared grief and understanding in these pages.

If you are looking for God in the cracks of your life, I hope you will find glimmers of the Light here that will lead you on to greater revelations. From the language of my written prayers, I hope you will make your own language of approach and take courage from my belief that we are never separate from God's love, no matter how distant it may feel. With Rilke, I affirm that "no feeling is final." I hope for better answers, more light, and more healing for all of us. And, above all things, for the courage to keep going.

(After) the fall

Seeking sight? Sit here.

I do not want
to look

at the beautiful
things

of this world
with

damaged eyes.
I do not

want to feel my
cells strain,

squint to interpret
the simplest

stimulus—like light.
I do not

want to look with
alien

mind, no longer
perceive what

I once could—
particles

Elizabeth Pinborough

of light and air,
waves of

sound, and clear,
ringing

bells of beauty
all around.

But now

a tin crackle pings
my ear

with oscillating pain.
Pitch

without tune, sound
sans

interpretation. Only
a brain

pleading: the world
is Fire—

why can no one
see?

heortleas (without heart)

My heart talks
to my brain,

to comfort her.
Heart is lesser,

but talks more.
The brain just

listens, and feels
wisdom working

through love's pulse.

I think the hit to my
head unclasped their

hands a measure,
such that to simply

stand was to feel
the rapid beating,

the desperate call
of one lost friend

to another.

Elizabeth Pinborough

Delta Waves Confuse & Befuddle

My
body
is all I have—
the remnants
of my memory are
buried in
b
ro
ke
n
ax ons,
scarred glia.
Electrochemical catastrophe is a
timeless
cascade of
arch   ing del   ta
wa   ves.

Even in
daylight.
Yes, the pure darkness of
day
li
gh
t
.

Truth with White Teeth Says, "Hello."

I walked out of the bookstore
today, and greeted

a spectacular Truth, smiling
with sharp white teeth:

"Hello," she whispered, grin
beginning to grow,

Hello, I spat back, brittle
slow.

"Although your limbs move like
sap dripping from

tree gash, although
your 3lb tofu

computer cannot orient among
a hewn forest

of slain neurons. Even though
your hands

are dropping dropping many
pieces you try to hold—

Elizabeth Pinborough

books trust memories thought
love sanctuary home;

Although, your spine is skewed,
neck compressed,

Back aching and nerves shot
painthrough,

Hello.

As the proud, wrinkled man
sports a blue hat

lettered 'Vietnam' (war smashed
his psyche, you know?),

as he wears golden pins declaring
valor, Perspective,

You wear your body, *your* red badge
of courage."

Hell.
O.

How to Remember the Word *Egg*.

Open the fridge, and find
a drawer.

Within it you might see celery
stalks, wrapped

in a plastic sleeve, crisp,
springreen, ready

to snap between your teeth.
Imagine raisins

on a concave, slathered with peanut
butter . . . . . .

Now, you're in first grade, unpacking
your lunch,

Oh! Ants on a log. You are
delighted when

you unfold love printed on a
paper towel.

"I love you, xo Mom," it reads,
enclosed within

Elizabeth Pinborough

an inky heart. Alone at a table
of many,

most with sweeter lunches
than yours

(Kit Kats and sugared cereals),
you still

know you're loved.
You know.

But, listen. The story of Humpty
Dumpty always

makes you sad with a kind of
nameless ache,

a kind of visceral, grown-up grief
each time

you think of all the king's
horses, men

trying to mend a shattered
egg.

Perhaps my brain is a star

Orion tilts
eastward toward
Mount Olympus. His
arms stretch the bowstring
to hunt the moon, stoic on our

shared horizon.
On earth, grief divides
within me almost like hunger,
into cristae—engines of emotional
energy folded in every brain cell. I have

little patience
for poetry any more.
I barely care to breathe. Beneath
layers of bone and matter—(dura, pia)—
and blood vessels, behold her grey, then

white at her core.
(Perhaps my brain is a star.)
O Jello-mama babe beauty curling
into fold upon fold of being. O lacy
cerebellum! Roundly estuarial, full of

Elizabeth Pinborough

dendritic greenwood.
O object of closest proximity,
my greatest delight. Endless, quaking,
scintillating with beingness, light and mind—
consciousness—I am cosmos talking to herself.

I bloomed from
the spark. O little flint!
Zinc exits ovum—becomes *poesis*—
from free association, from costly speech,
from that which cannot be spoken, cannot be named.

Elizabeth Pinborough

February 21, 2020
5 years to the day of my first death

Grief, mistress of memory,
       walks with me now
       clothed in gray
       garments.

My funerary hymn is no
       melody, but howl.
       Not glorious—
       grim.

She tames my triumphs with
       her low instruments:
       double bass, contra-
       bassoon.

Didgeridoo pulses a heartbeat
       of air, recalls every
       throbbing beat of
       pain,

every absurd alteration to my body
and brain. I did not want
to serve her
today.

I wanted to revel in neuroplastic
change—the speed found,
pain allayed, poeming
again.

Please hear me, soft one, you
will always be there
with me in the
shadows.

Elizabeth Pinborough

Her longing,

for poetry? Is dim. Shy woman, she lives in dusk, still.

Her nest is neither new, nor old. Perhaps neither made nor unmade.

She is swamp companion, whose nets are crafted with chapped fingers, uncertain musculature, frozen fascia—

With these she catches the soursweet whorls of everyone's trash.

"I believe," she says, "I hear them," the words made fecund in stagnant water.

Her hopes of uncoiling a self tightly folded in upon itself, again? Slim.

At this, she can't help but feel grief shard across her temporal bone, like myriad hooks barbing fish muscles
we will eat.

Unwind (or is it un-wound?) the self.

Unmake, reprogram, reconstruct, reconstrue the whole blasted endeavor.

Untwist the strands of maternal and paternal making. Begin again from embryo.

Bodycells quiver with old knowings, dead frequencies of feelings and disease, and like she would with minnows in the murky seas of her mind, she releases them one
by
one—
gives them over to the greater light.

A broken psalm on

When life-the-death
comes racing along,
when death-become-life
is a distant song,

dash to the depths that   howl   er.
Crash to the heights with a   y   o   w   l
and fist and *pound* to the ground
all littleness,
all middle
****

mess, crumble
tumble rumble
over-
down.

Because just you.
No more,
no less.

When poem rings bleak (or worse, cliché)
and you just haven't got the words to

say,
or maybe there are too many
of the wrong ones,
day after damn
day—

Humble the bumbler with humility's cry: after all,
you DID try.

Elizabeth Pinborough

Today, be gentle

with your self.

She has brought you here, by whatever
means necessary.

Acknowledge her. Thank her.
Attend to her.

She is wise
(wisdom can mean stepping down).

She is brave
(brave can be sitting out).

She is sure
(even sure that she does not know).

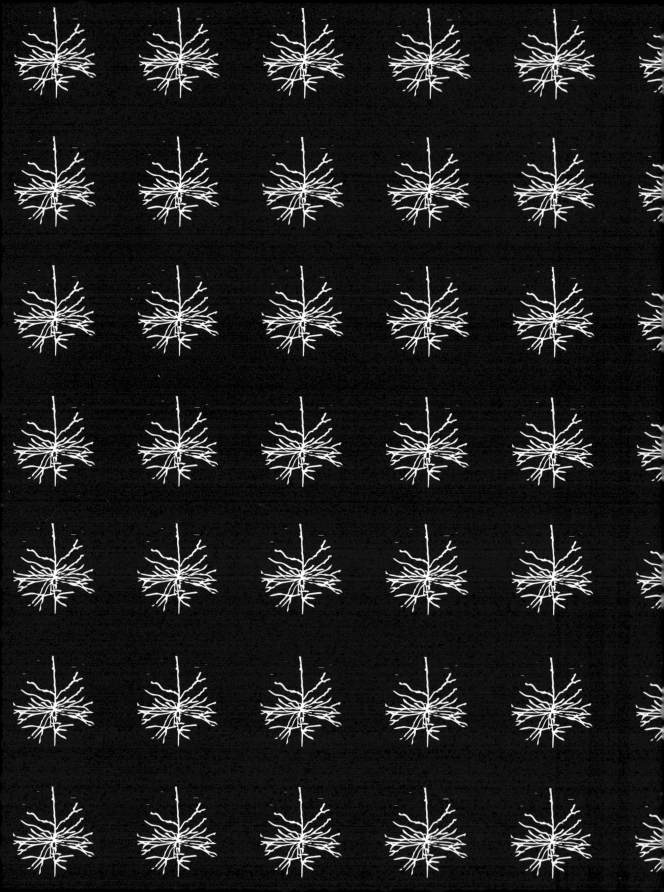

Perhaps lament

When you're called to be sick and not well,
when you're called to mourn, not rejoice,
when you're called to sit in sackcloth and ash,
not splendorous robes.

When the ache of days
fades to the ache of night, when friends
become foes and foes strike in their might, when God beats
a distant drum and doesn't warm the hearth, when sweet
becomes bitter
and heart wilts with fright—

angels are watching from the wings.

And perhaps they bear up the most unspeakable things and.
  Perhaps
they lift up the most sorrowful songs and breathe
breaths of life into the weariest lungs.

And perhaps they draw maps in the stars
and desperately beckon:
look, here's where you are. Here's God's throne.

It's not that far.

Elizabeth Pinborough

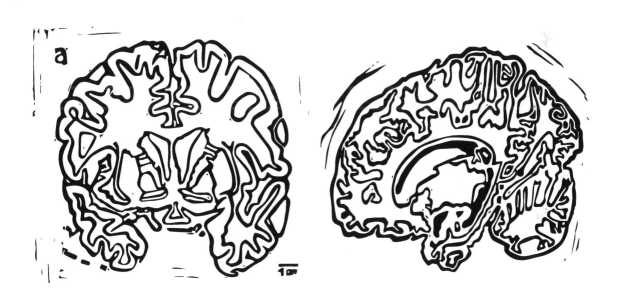

tigress to tiger

I have gone

into

a

s

m

a

l

l

place.

Experts call it
"freeze,"
"dissociation."

My gait is rigid.
When I sit, I curl
around my core.

Do. not. move.

He (*stripes, tooth,
claw*)
is waiting.

Elizabeth Pinborough

poetry does return

Dear blossoms broke.
Little pathways bloomed
for a time and then, weedrun,
shook.

Prune, weep, prune, until
again, soon, little buds
make room.

Seeds sunk to heartwells,
stems struck with thorn,
shorn to cuttings.
Lorn.

Remember, then, and
don't forget,
inkpen and heart.

Write the word so
one day you, too, shall
complete the craft—
We have conquered.

Metamorphosis

1 Samuel 14:27

Before bees encombed
my viscera in honeyed
hexagons,

I, Lioness, lay down
to die. (To be eaten,
certainly, by wind,

sand—*gradual erasure*—
surely.

Not rent by a warrior's
hands in my vineyard).

Opaque grapes—blackened blue—hang

from greening vines
above; the tearing is (not?)
unbearable—(being ripped

by fingers into halves
feels like being born).

Elizabeth Pinborough

A swarm of stinging sensations
follows. I rot in the sun,
a bleeding apiary.

He comes again,
carves wax from the
cavity—now empty
& full—

he palms the oozing cells till
they drip with gold.
My pain is Samson's provender—

my muscles make a sweet
meat, sanguine ichor for his
mother. At dinner, I am a riddle.

How could she who eats
be food, someone strong
so sweet?

The people reason
(to no avail). Their minds
can't catch the riddle's

tail: how does death come
to a maiden before her
time?

How does a ram's horn
signal the moon's
decline (or a battle cry)?

How does a man who dips
his staff in forbidden honey
still live, enlightenment

tearing at his eyes?

Elizabeth Pinborough

Elizabeth Pinborough

The Brain's Lectionary

I.
And if my brain dances
in her own twilit wild,

    singing

(with gown torn, raving)
a hymn of

    shame,

then I will be found on
the causeway to a

    salted lake

where buffalo brush
purple skeins of sky,

    holding

my camera out the
window.

II.

And if

my brain spins doubt
and death with planetary

force,

then I will be found
climbing canyons,

arms

cast up to an invisible
sphere of angels & stars,

praying

without belief, hoping
without hope.

Elizabeth Pinborough

III.

And if

all is not enough to bring
my throbbing brain back to

proper

form, if healing unscrolls
neurons as quickly as I

reroll

them, if atoms draw apart
in final uncertainty,

then

I will be found accounting
to *nephesh* what is *nephesh*.

I will be

found. I will be found.
I will be found.

what happens

when there's room
for *you*, again?
what happens

when each moment
is more than you stuck
on most painful pin

of dysregulation?

what happens
when you rise
and move without

unbearable suspension
of arms & legs & intention?

what happens
when you rise
not to weep,

but rather rejoice?

Elizabeth Pinborough

you still cry.

then

grief comes, cloaked
in softest gray wool,
bearing a bowl of bright
apples.

Remember the fruit, she says.
Remember the fall.

Elizabeth Pinborough

... Oceans ...

Pseudoliparis swirei

Mariana Trench
                scythes through
                                Pacific depths,
                                        where
                        snailfish trim
                ghostfins
like sails.
                These ghostkin
                                float, flat
                                        ethereal
                        bodies filled
                with extra-
terrestrial
                motion.
                                Their haunted
                                        bodies
                        glide through
                the black
crevasse—
                the furthest
                                dive to a

Elizabeth Pinborough

longing
for light.
But I tell
you—the trenches
are deeper
than ocean's
lowest
point, deeper
than deep space,
deeper even
than death.
I cannot
pretend
to know
answers
while writing
poems on
a dead life.
Here,
my pen
cannot
save me.

Big Bang Neurogenesis

In the wake, astrocytes died, burning cells decayed close
to nothing. Remains (enrobed, enraged) emerged as new
matter—a kind I cannot see but know

> to name since stars spin alike at center and
> circumference in galaxies hugging collapsed suns.
> Gravitational globes, invisible jars, collect star shards into
> shapes:

spirals, ellipses, embryos suspended in dark amber. Space
pauses her expansion to watch: the Milky Way, fully
fluorescent with algae caught in tide pool's tumbler.

> After the quake, stem cells amass as neurospheres
> to patch gaps in brain's starfields. Neurons reach,
> branches longing universe wide for connection after
> explosion,

humming hymns to bend trees into lights massive enough to
see, massive enough to feel.

Elizabeth Pinborough

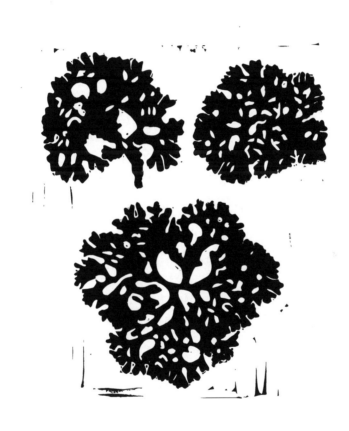

Elizabeth Pinborough

From One Great Cleaving Rock

Waves—
        parabolas of turquoise light,
        fold self on self on self, tangling
        seaweed into clumps of mind.

Shells—
        laminated pearl with memory,
        tumble, empty of consequential
        bodies, vacant mineral rage.

Fissures—
        from one great cleaving rock,
        open; magma exudes, cools
        to glass, the core's only regret.

Grief visits again (*swim, girl, swim*)

clothed in the sea.
Your red cap is fit for
swimming now.
Dive in, she bids.

Her waters are
purple. Your hopes
were aquamarine.
You always envisioned

yourself standing in glassen
transparencies revealing
crimson starfish on white sands,

not as Gertrude Ederle in goggles
and black silk departing Cap Gris-Nez.

You are swimming the
Channel for Kingsdown,
now. You—one tiny atom of
humanity—will surely meet

Elizabeth Pinborough

the flood with all the bravery
of a child flinging herself
at rope's end into
the river.
Swim,
girl,
swim.

Dorcas Resurrexit

Acts 9:36–43

Women in the upper room:

> See, these are they that she made
> while in the land of the living.
> Behold her delicate stitching, each
> stitch created with exactness, an
> emblem of her righteousness.

Dorcas:

> I shed my frail frame and swam
> off into space. I seemed to be
> walking through water, the air
> was so thick. I noticed others
> walking, walking through water.

Women in the upper room:

> It was too soon. It is too soon.
> We are bereft without her. Who
> will stitch our lives together,
> sackcloth and silk? Who will give
> our alms to the poor?

Elizabeth Pinborough

Dorcas:

> These bodies glow as they go,
> walking above the earth. They
> are being drawn above. Below
> me, houses spill down to the sea.

First woman:

> I bathed her hands and feet.

Second woman:

> I bathed her legs.

Third woman:

> I bathed her arms and breast.

Women in the upper room:

> I, we, anointed her head.

Dorcas:

> I spy a glittering soul tossed by
> the threshing waves. My spirit
> arabesques into water. I swim,
> but her glint is gone.

Women in the upper room:

> We hear there is one in a nearby
> town who can conjure the dead

by a mysterious power—
some even call it divine.

Peter:

I am called to the sea. From
the street I hear the weeping
women. Noxious air hangs in
the stairwell. I walk the stairs,
stone upon stone; light glimmers
in my solar plexus.

First woman:

I clapped my hands and raised
them up.

Second woman:

I walked the floor with laboring
steps.

Third woman:

I held her garments to my breast
and counted each stitch.

Peter:

I am climbing a sacred mountain.

Elizabeth Pinborough

Dorcas:

> I . . . I.

Women in the upper room:

> She swiftly goes, is gone.

— – —

Dorcas:

> Nets float like veined branches.
> Figures swim among the cerulean
> forest dark. These are not fish,
>
> but something else. They are circling,
> circling, their black jaws snapping.
> The candle burning in my breast
> flashes, then dims.

Peter:

> Within this room three women
> spin in three tremulous, jolting
> orbits.

Women in the upper room:

> He slowly comes, is come, the
> man who walks as in a dream.

Third woman:

> Sir, our sister fled—trailing
> darkling silken threads.

Second woman:

> In each face she sought the
> Mourn'd One.

First woman:

> Now she seeks Him, the
> Veil'd One.

Peter:

> Spectral orbs whirl amid
> woolen blues and linen greens.
> Planetary voices clamor and
> babble.
>
> As words escape they singe
> my throat—*All depart.*

— – —

Women on the upper stair:

> We are banished. We are shut
> out. The door is closed before
> us. Death hangs all around us.

Elizabeth Pinborough

Dorcas:

> The figures cast and catch me
> with nets. Their clawed fingers
> snatch at my weedy dress.

> *Pull, pulls, the undertow. Howl,*
> *howls, their wailsome song.*

Peter, on the Sea of Galilee:

> Our boat is rocking. Onyx
> sky hurtles above, tinged
> with white points of light.
> Onyx waves curl beneath us.

> He comes walking, walking on
> the onyx waves. Beckoned, I
> slip my legs over the ship's
> side.

> I sink; adamantine waters crush
> my heels. I plead, yet He lifts
> me up.

Women on the upper stair:

> We fear we are lost without her.

Dorcas:

> A golden laver floats up from the
> deep, wreathed by dancing diamond
> bangles and scroll-engraved rings.

> Templed riches entomb me—the silver
> menorah toppled and swept by Mediterranea
> to Italia and back, a wildly rocking ark,
> and rusty cherubim.

Peter:

> On the mount, I pluck a dusty asphodel,
> white petals shocked with red. Asphodel
> seeds spill, like grain, into my palm. I cast
> them on the air.

> Eddies rive my mind; a shrouded corpse
> appears standing on the sand.

Women on the upper stair:

> O . . . O!

Peter:

> Music throbs around my temples. Ah!
> Verdure springs from the floorboards.

> Upon the green-glenned floor I kneel.

Elizabeth Pinborough

Streams flicker past my heels, and from
a corner birds whisper in unknown
tongues.

I cast my mind and soul, weft and
warp, into the sea, the sea I walked
at Galilee. *Come, daughter of the desert.*
Come, maiden of the sand. Rise up
and seek the living stream.

Women on the upper stair:
Follow the glowing thread, dear one.
Follow it with all your might.

Peter:
My net is cast. Will she come?

— – —

Dorcas:
A distant word thrums in my ears;
the wailing ones writhe, and disappear.
I shake the nacreous chains of death.

Like a bow-struck arrow my spirit rises.

The sea surface shatters. I am Helios
splitting oceanic night. A gazelle, I fly
across the Negev. My feet beat the air,
my heart pants for day.

Women on the upper stair:

Our eyes are heavy with sleep. Stones sit
upon our eyelids.

Peter:

I do not welcome this dark morning.

Dorcas:

Shadowed and blue, the house is silent.
Through labyrinthine streets I am come
to the door, pulled as though by a fine
gold wire.

Here are my dears, asleep on the stair,
clutching pieces of my cloth. I smooth
the hair back from their faces.

I enter.

First woman:

I feel a wind!

Elizabeth Pinborough

Second woman:
> My hem rustles.

Third woman:
> My temples cool.

Peter:
> The bedclothes stir. A woman stands
> hesitant in the air.

Dorcas:
> A man is slumped on my bedroom floor,
> a piece of flotsam washed up after a
> storm.
>
> My body lies crumpled, a fleshly piece of
> cloth. To step in again, to take up this
> robe again—do I dare?

— - —

Women near the upper door:
> Something stirs within.

— - —

Dorcas:

> My eyes crack like searing coals. Violets
> twinge my tongue. A coin cools my burning
> lips.

> Palm leaves fringe the floor beneath my bed.
> At my feet the flotsam man contemplates.
> We are suspended in reverence—I the living
> altar, he a living sacrifice.

> A cock crows and mars our peace. The man
> swiftly goes, is gone.

> The women press in, shivering about my bed
> like wind-plucked fronds. Clucking softly they
> touch me with feathery fingers.

First woman:

> I caress her cheek, taut and warm like a
> cow's belly.

Second woman:

> I listen to her breathe, the breaking
> of waves.

Third woman:

> I stroke her red locks, a crown of fire.

Elizabeth Pinborough

Peter:

The sun strikes the city, scattering fish scales profligately on stones. She is unsurpassed, an earthly city of fishers and men.

Her market quivers with life like Solomon's Portico. Here no one crawls within my shadow for a miracle. Here I am a stranger, an unremarkable wanderer.

Here I lay aside my nets and walk into the sea.

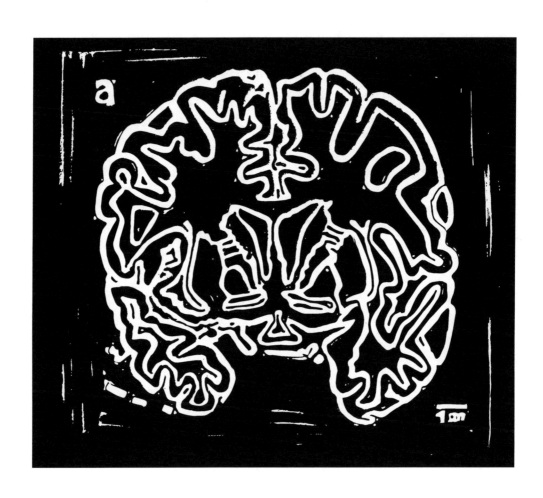

Elizabeth Pinborough

Autophagy

I accidentally gave my brain a feast
of itself—dying neurons divided up
as scraps to be nibbled away after
the collapse. How odd, how unholy,
cells glutting themselves with memories—
a childhood, my neighbor, dislodged
hours—a frenzy of krill skimming
algae from Antarctic seas.

Fact: Autophagy is expected—neuroplastic, even.
Novelty furrows and refurrows neural
dirt, paths ready to be traveled with recall,
or abandoned like ancient earthworks
aligned with the moon.

Elizabeth Pinborough

Jared Answers

Ether 2:23

Give me blue paths, bioluminescence
across the waters. Give me constellations
dotting firefly squid. Give me cathedrals
of waves, sunlight shafts, twisted
seaweed columns. Give me clerestories
of comb jellies, rainbow-backed candles.
Give me a dolphin diaconate, incense
churning in its wake. Give me sanctified
sharks, resurrected fish, scales wrapped
in undying light. Give me a universe
microscopic, dinoflagellates flashing on,
off. Give me algal blooms, lanternfish,
echolocation. Give me pods of mother
belugas clicking to their calves. Give me
bellstruck glaciers groaning, big ships
cracking underwater. Give me the brains
of sperm whales, guided by earth's
electromagnetic beacons. Give me coral
that glows fuschia, and a blue whale's heart.
Or, take trilobite fossils—make exoskeletons
shimmer. God, please, touch these
stones till they glow as sea glass.

{tiny} Lights

Welcome to the hinterlands

Your hintermind is here
in moonless pools
of unfamiliar
fish.

Saints pass this way.
Sages scry the
waves—

thorn,

Angel—

are you alive,
or are you dead?
What do you take
for compass
Rose?

Elizabeth Pinborough

Can you
navigate by tiniest lights:
phytoplankton under microscope, <.> <.>
neuron blinking   -

                    -      -   -

stem   -   -   -   -   -
one thousand   -   -   -
one   -
two one thousand
two
cell

into life?

When self capsizes, dear swimmer,
is north still North?

Which star, which horizon, do you
set your sextant by?

Are algae enough to guide
you home?

Silver Lake

The mountain ridge glows ochre
before night hides her, tarnished

silver shivering with stars. Her
waters are my telescope. Dusk

scrims quasars, light stretched
red by time. These mark the

earliest abyss, brimming with
suns, quivering millions. Still,

I will never see the aching edge,
even of this world—nevermind

fields of neon galaxies swarming
like insects eating a rim around the

universe. Make way for a silver
lake, they say, lapping at the shore.

Elizabeth Pinborough

Ekphrasis on a sagittal brain slice by Drs. Greg Dunn & Brian Edwards

I could worship you,
            deepest goldenbright
                        byways of mind
                                    encoded in

liquid silver lines s   g   s
                    h   n   c
                i   i   o   e   r
                    m   r   n   h   e   n
                    m e   t   e   .

Neurological mysteries
            are micoetched and
                        inexhaustible
                                    gilded ridges.

I could climb each
            electric thread
                        and slide into
                                    squishy sulci—

savor a sacred swish,
            of knowledge kept
                        in the brilliant
                                    bodymind.

If I could but
    caress keenest
        beryl cerebellum,
            magenta mysterium,

I would find
    Her there,
        I would find
            Her maidens

robed in astrocytes
    garbed in glia,
        shawled with
            stem cells.

Elizabeth Pinborough

                                                                            We
                                                                    never
                                                            have
                                                    seen
                                            our
                                    strong
                            God
                        (curled
                in
            the
        cranial
cavity)

We   never   have   never   seen   Her

with so much *light*,
                Her almost
                                    unbearable
                                            radiance.

Purkinje ekphrasis

Dana Simmons
Warholizes brain
cells.

Her neurological
art glows neon
under

the microscope,
Purkinje cells
edited

with color contrast.
Psychedelic
science

years beyond Ramón
y Cajal's and
Camillo

Golgi's Prix Nobel
still requires
analog

Elizabeth Pinborough

attention—isolate
cell, dye,
record.

Here we are, a century
later, imaging
self,

imaging branching
organs of
sense

with skillful hands,
micropipettes,
fluorescence.

Purkinje looks like
a little heart,
leafing

from aorta into
seaweed
fronds.

Dr. Simmons pictures
the cerebellar
forest,

notes the pattern
of lightning,
antlers,

and all manner
of organic
matter,

where holons are
roots are
all.

Now I know better
what the man in
Bethsaida

meant when he saw
trees as men
walking.

Elizabeth Pinborough

Collect for Neurogenesis

Spell the name of each new neuron:
I am E l e c t r o n, radical, free.
Now A t o m, who divides, decrees death,
a l i v e with charge and might.

This one, e l e c t r i c i t y—
w a v e   l e n g t h s
of magnitudes
crinkling across
cortices Beta a l p h a t   h e t a   d   e   l   t   a   (omega)

Little & many branches of the - - - - -
                              T - - - - - - - - -
              - - - - - - R
                          E - - - -
                          E   s
                          a r e
              s   t
              i   y
      r   . . .   n
  d   . . .   . a
 s e e k i n g   . .   .   . .   s p a c e s   &
    e   . . .   .   a   .   inter s tices
 d   i   .   t   . . .   . . .   e
 . . .   . s &
 . .   .   r   .   .   . .
 .   t   i   o   . . .
 s   .   b   e   i   . . . .   .   .   n .
 .   f   ngne   s   s   .   s
 o   e .
                                                                 s

D u s k crusts leaves
        with
                C O P P E R
                light, speaking all manner of deep illusions.

Call us c o n n e c t - t o m e—map of each

                           .   .   switch,   .

      gate,   . ^   .

      .   .   .   .   ^

     .   .   ^   . and

  way   .   >   .   .   .   >   point

                 .   .   .   .

  .   > .   .   .   >. .   .   .

.   .   .   . .   <   .   .   .   .   .

. on the quadrillionth road that leads to conscious Y O U—   .   .   . .

.   .   .   .

. .   .   .

.   . . A fabulous sparking universe of .   . . ^ .. ^ .. ^   . .   binaries.

. .   .   .   ^   .

.   .   .   . ^   .   .   .

  . Assent   .   .   .   .   .   . brings

      consent   . > .   .   .   .   Denial

      embraces   .   fibs . . . .

        Gravity   harrows In . . . .

          ^   ^ carnation-JOLTed

        ^   ^

        Knowledge, lost

        Mental nodes

        Open pulses,

         Quickening

         Roars singing

         Tumultuous

          Undone!

         Verify

         X-ray

         Yawn—

          ZAP!

We are c e r e b r u m.
We are b r a i n.
We are begun.

Photo 51

I.

Like a head of wheat, Her golden strands loop eternally.
Like Morse dit-datting over the airwaves, bringing news of war,
reports from the bloody front lines, the crisp clip of letters is
evident, spelling fingernails and hair, age and appearance.
These are the constitutive stars, the building stones of nations
within one soul.

II.

    Each luminescent   globe spins,

        fiery pearls   suspended

          opposite   her sisters.

              They swirl,
             in depths of
            hollow light.

        Rosalind   Franklin

      first saw the   structure,

    photoed the X   on tiny glass.

Elizabeth Pinborough

III.

When adenine and thymine decouple,
and guanine and cytosine decay,
who will revive us?
I will, I seem to
hear Her say.

IV.

Take this leaf here and form a poultice. *See?*

Spread it on the wound, the bone where star fragments scattered. *Can you hear the dying dust?*

She now sings the songs of creation. *Eulalia Eulay!*

She sings of capillaries entwining each bone, of lymph clearing each node. *Breathe.*

She's singing of nerves spinning out electrochemical pulse, serving out feeling, sensation, thought, and verse.

And if you listen, with all your ears, she sings of the Code. *Sisters, hear.*

Come to this, the altar, the anchor. This, the Golden Braid. *Come, let us speak of Resurrection morning.*

Klaus, the Diatomist, navigates by light of phytoplankton

They rise, great sweeping swaths of
swarming waters, *phosphorescing*.
(Or, perhaps, they cluster in a local
gutter—workmanlike, mundane.)

Every shade of bluesweet and tourmaline
green, these diatoms dye the photic zone
with turquoise lights
visible to orbiting astronauts.

In an oceanic gloaming they keep us
alive by digesting carbon dioxide—
their record, our breaths, their trace,
our homeostasis.

Beyond the reach of an unaided eye
(outgrowth of the brain,
packed with diatoms of her own—
the rods, the cones),

Klaus Kemp fashions microscopic mandalas,
radiating triangular and emerald,
each alga a planktonic jewel, a single cell,
singular silica shell—

Elizabeth Pinborough

singular glow on needle's end.

"We are now dealing in microns of movement,"
he says, narrating the exacting
arrangement on glass slides. "This is where
the dexterity comes in."

A minuscule star orbits in the center place,
followed by filaments,
wheels, dulcimers and an X-marks-the-spot.
Thousands of varieties

more populate the pages of his record books,
an obsessive collection
of earthy spheres, invisible lives, miraculous
micro-architectures.

Does he guess at their meaning, weighing
weightless creatures against the great scheme?
Or does he merely place them into patterns,
beautiful but mute?

What do *you* discover, then, in diatomaceous soil,
dear poet? Observable universes? Organic salvation?
Microbial memory? Brittle cosmologies? Or bits of fossil,
gristle for your toothpaste.

Elizabeth Pinborough

Emily—as Envisioned

.

Her pencil
scratches
on a scrap
while bread
bakes to fill
the box—

The rye crusts,
reasons rising
in steamy Plumes
from oven
crumbs—

She, the white-
frocked mouse
Scribbling against
rapacious Sun,
bundles real
into oppositions,
while rumbling
Death

rolls the streets
of Amherst.

Damned be the
worldbuilders—
She chides
in Graphite Line—
Listen to One
Black Buzz
spluttering
on a Window
Sill.

— – —

Then

When All is Silent—
in the House,
a Garden of Infinite
pages of Leaves
grows across
Thresholds,
Papering the walls
& coffering the ceiling.

Elizabeth Pinborough

Waspy Figs Husk
Open, and . . .
Seeds splay in
Ruinous Red &
Yellow Contrapunto on
The table—

Here is *Magnolia*,
Princely, proud.
And *Calendula*, where
Lepidoptera play.

She wanders her
Interior Garden, fastening
Flowers to Papers,
each petal scribed in Latin,
A sun-hatched Herbarium
on a Butcher Block—

Or, so I imagine.

— – —

Coaxing Chords
from the Piano
is my *tiny* communion.

I clink—and clatter,
pound and Play.

We whisper through
the Kitchen door—
Botanical Egress shut
& exit barred.

She sends me
Strange Verses
from her Land—
Paper Coals
and Burning Ink
Brighten the Void.

We are sisters,
joined Umbilical.

No machine
Mind mediates
Ours—

— – —

I wish to observe her
Cranium Thrumming,
crackling with Frequencies

Elizabeth Pinborough

snatched by Ossicles, &
transmitted by quaking hairs
to her Brain—

To meet the Woman who
scribbled the World
so small she
cracked it open
with double syllable—
Be • cause.

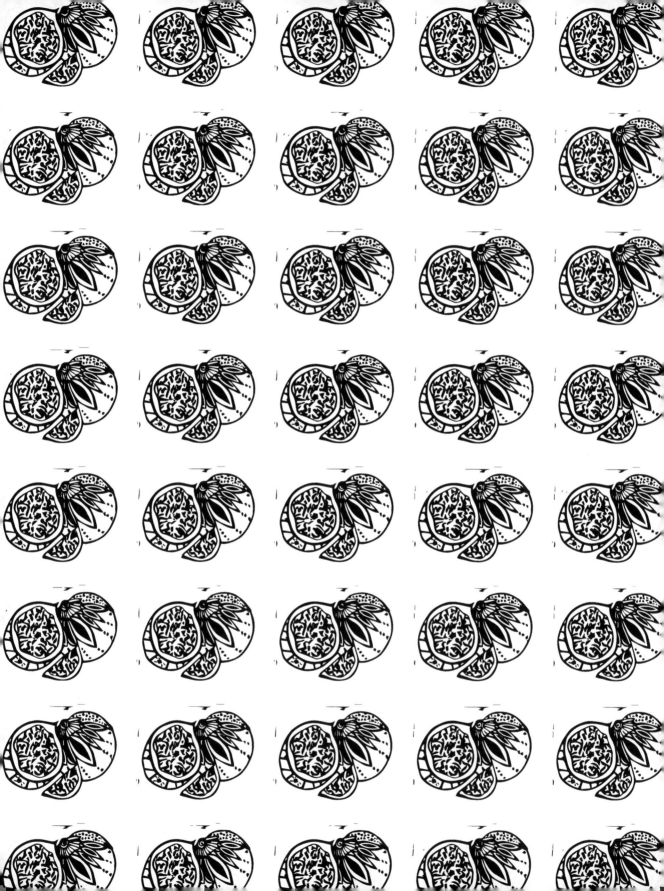

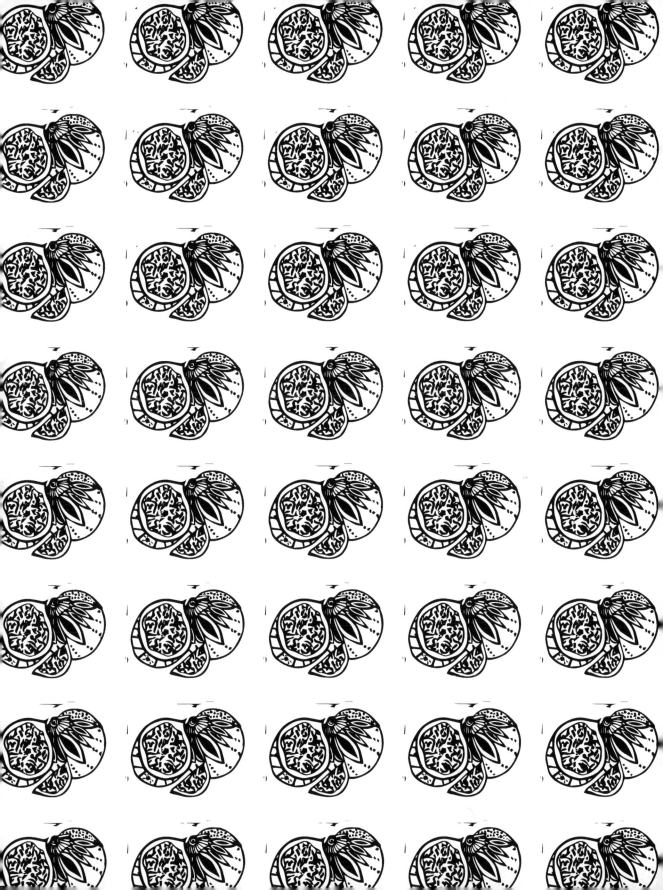

To symbolize God would be impossible:

God is not a symbol.
My brain symbolizes

God God God God

                                                s

through God's myriad—   e   c r o c o d i l e s....
works of   d   e
                          i   n
organic form & shape   r   t
& matter—like   r   n   ....
               i   a
         m   t
      u e a o   i
    l   m t u   o
   l   o   r   n   n
I   r   i   t   s.
         i   c   a   .....
Consensus: e   e   n
        s....   s.   s.
God creates infinite trillions   ....
of living holograms,

Elizabeth Pinborough

the minds of humankind.
I compute experiences—

not equations, not math.   Exactly, not.
Mathematics come after

p o t e n t i a t i o n s of input code
sensory delights, electromagnetic

phenomena outside my eye.
Still, the eyeball comes (.) (.)

walking.

Healing the Brain>>>

Sometimes the psalmist clasps her own heart

These days,
when I wake, my
hand is often on
my heart.

It's as if
my subconscious
knows the
brokenness of being
in this world
and bids my aching
body,

Be
healed.

Elizabeth Pinborough

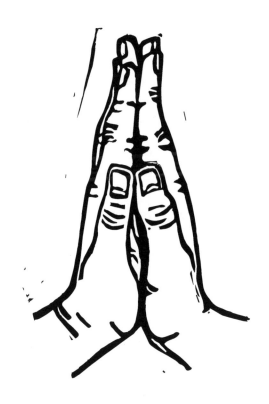

hope, a

thing with pages

Notes interline future days

with turquoise, hummingbirds,

& ancient caves. Here your words

lie yet undiscovered, scrolls and

scrolls, wrapped with leather.

Dig, scribe,

unroll.

Elizabeth Pinborough

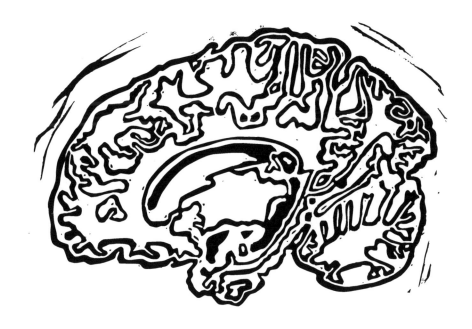

The Brain's Lectionary

A guide to healing

1.
To mollify pain,
  I picture colors, shapes.
                Then
    remove each artifact
from my brain:
halberd and helmet,
    plates of smelted
                iron,
    boulders & nets,
serpents & insects.
A primeval knife
    stabs my right parietal
                lobe,
    slices straight through
  my corpus | callosum,
an unnecessary (*invisible*)
    incision.

— – —

Elizabeth Pinborough

2.
The colors exposed are
        what I expect:
                                rust
        hides magma rock,
next, oozy chartreuse.
A layer of ecru
        appears (gauze before
                                wound)
        then very pulp of person-
hood is revealed.
The bodyworker
        inquires, holding my
                                head,
        Did you have surgery?
No, I said. Each
fracture's unseen.

— – —

3.
Now my skull,
      relic of self, shatters
                    seven
      times. Holy basil
blooms, bearing
medicines in Her
      leaves. *One morning,*
                  you

      will rise, she says,
draped in seaweed
fronds as with a
      shroud, to meet
                  yourself.

      Around my neck
she loops the beads,
speaks her prayer,
      Amen.

Elizabeth Pinborough

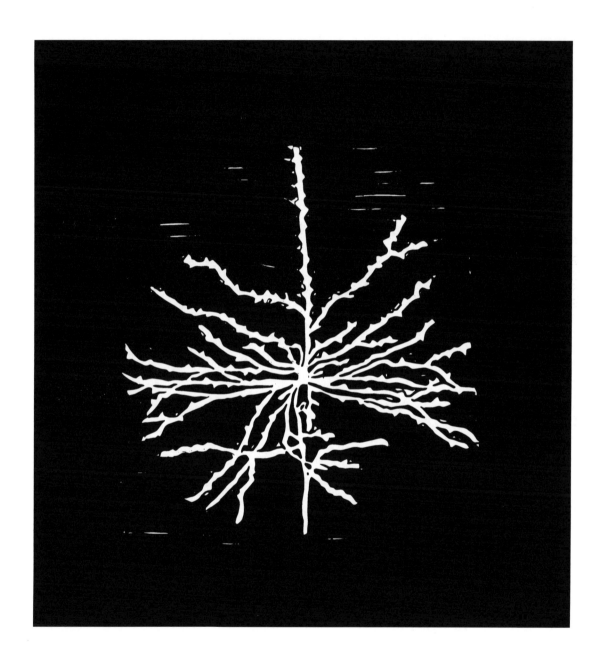

Elizabeth Pinborough

A Psalm for - - - - - - - -

Pray the fine, clear line   -   -   -   -   in one continuous prayer.
Pray the sinuous verse,-   -   -   and the short.
Pray the pause   -   - -   before revision,
Pray the mystery   -   -   before revelation.
Pray the thought   -   -   -   back into thinking.
Pray the blood   -   -   -   back into flowing.
Pray the CSF -   -   -   -   -   move unobstructed.
Pray the vertebrae   -   -   -   be sentinel soldiers.
Pray the time stretch,   -   -   -   then stretch again.
Pray the vagus nerve   -   -   plump, restore her form.
Pray the nerves relax,   -   -   neurotransmitters transmit.

Pray the hole be filled- - - - -   -   -   -   -   -   -   -   -
the gaps,   -   mended, gentle
words

returned unended, rather than these bloody - paper - bullets -
of - the - brain.

Unfold, friends

I buy books (and many),
line my shelves with
sheafs and leaves—
spines red and lettered
gold.

I let them sit, *A Velocity
of Being* rubbing shoulders
with *Approaching Zion*.
Ancient *Thames* touches
Ethics and Infinity.

I behold their holy witness,
their many pearls waiting
to be discovered, dust them
off after years of grit
from the bottom of my sea.

Bonaventure, Mary Oliver,
Layli Long Soldier—may
I say, thank you?
What were scabs, scars,
fissures, & tears—

Elizabeth Pinborough

insect landscapes & grasslands—
populate my shelves as
bound and written
down transformations.
Awake, they say,

arise—thy time
has come.

print and be done with it already

Just   think of all that's been printed—Budgets in red or
black &   brochures for forgotten museums of ammonites.
Think of   white tickets for tart plays, Programs purple
and gloss   for *Swan Lake* curled in hot hands or rolled
into tubes, as   your makeshift binoculars. Remember the
car ads beside   symphony sponsors, lavish spreads of
jewelry hawkers,   magazines minding every answer
money can buy, and   editorials, hot-under-the-collar
editorials, setting newsprint   aflame. Doctor bills arrive
clad in deceptively gentle blue,   receipts showing you've
purchased healing. Casual catalogues   of cowboy boots
clutter your mailbox, while comics crinkle   in the yellow
Sunday funnies. Don't you think there's room   among the
floating flotsam and bobbing jetsam for your creations,   too?

Elizabeth Pinborough

Immediately

I saw a man once, clustered with people, walking
with multitudes. He had a certain glory about
him, the glow reserved only for little children
and those who have known great hardships.
The dust sprang up around his sandals
and clung to the hem of his garment.
A group of men, officious, intruding,
huddled near him, speaking to him.
And somehow he remained aloof.
I knew they could prevent me
from going near him, if I made
myself known. So I hung back
until the right moment and
flung myself to the ground.
Extending my hand—which
trembled a lot—I grasped
the cloth and kissed it.
I felt a shock go
straight to my
blood and heal
my inmost
wound.

Elizabeth Pinborough

The Psalmist Inquires, *Under what moon?*

Was it when, under waning gibbous,
the night-silver forceps
drew me sliverlike
from shadowed
womb,

fresh from other worlds,
a daughter of
Time?

Or was it when, under waxing crescent,
my head cracked a new-solar
edge of consciousness
and shafts
sliced

unholy carnage into
my brain, losing self in
dark matter?

Could it have been under the
rimrock round of lunar
canyons (fifty-two
cycles complete)

while Time-crucified
consciousness birthed
stars anew?

Now perhaps it is when, crescent waning,
my ghostly cranium crinkles,
onto the black screen, quiet
with osseous
light—

I am canny with thoughts,
knowing light *and*
time.

Elizabeth Pinborough

The things they carried—

The things they carried—
burdens invisible—

Words so finely scribed
in their DNA that
generations & generations
that held the books could
not perceive them—

These are the sacred
mysteries, the taboos,
the secrets, the untold
stories and sorrows
and songs.

We all become singers,
in our own time, before
we read the words
writ genetic: *You are
your family. And not.*

*You are
you.*

The code breaker.
The diviner.
The sage.

Spiral hearts

For my grandmother

Salty   blues   eddy
beneath   Haystack   Rock,
curling   into   basalt
pools of   anemones,   starfish.
Arms radiate fuschia,
remind me of Shirley,
her roses heavy with
bees. At Ecola   Point I watch
a bald eagle drift   on ocean updrafts
overhead. Chambered tides whorl songs in my blood.
Ache burns through my pericardium. My left ventricle finds
flame ascending aortic. O lonely huntress! Mournful wine
dampens neurons (*neon green multiplicities*). Electricities
stop. Grief imitates my heart's beats, seeks what she
cannot be—*beloved*—metes lack (lost luster), loves
my shadow-self, a sandy shell with cracked
mother of pearl. Grief becomes her own
longing, says, *Prepare to lose your
compass*. I do. Then I see
our twinned souls,
walking home,
together.

Elizabeth Pinborough

Together,
walking home,
our twinned souls,
compass. We do. Then, I see.
Longing says, *Prepare to lose your*
mother of pearl. Grief becomes her own,
my shadow-self, a white shell with cracked
cannot be. Beloved—metes lack (lost luster). Love
stops. Grief imitates her heart, beats in turn, seeks
electricity. O diving peregrine! Seven swords cut her
traces. She teaches electric flight, arias. . . . My sinoatrial
node lights, muscles contract. Chambered, tides whorl songs,
turquoise, coastal floods, grief gardening by the seaside.
A bald eagle drifts   on ocean updrafts,
bees. At Ecola   Point I watch
her roses, heavy with
reminders of Shirley.
Arms radiate fuschia,
pools of   anemones,   starfish.
Curling   into   basalt
beneath   Haystack   Rock,
salty   blues   eddy.

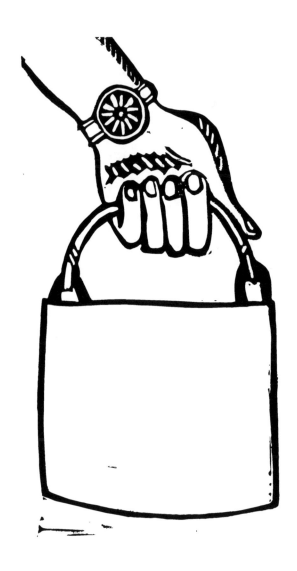

Elizabeth Pinborough

Wherein I see a solar eclipse

```
(((((((((((((((*)                                    (.))))))))))))))))
(((((((((((((((                                        ))))))))))))))
(((((((((((((                                           ))))))))))))
(((((((((((                                              ))))))))))
(((((((((                                                 ))))))))
(((((((                                                    )))))))
((((((                                                      ))))))
(((((              [flares]...]...]...] [obscured]          )))))
((((                                                         ))))
Sun                                                           )))
((                                                             ))
(                                                               )
captive to

         infinite [..........]

))))))))))))))
moonseeds              [   [ [  [ [[[wavering]] ] ]  ]    ]   ] [revealed]
))))))))))))))))

on t[he] stone-          [{caesura}] hewn

[...] stair of the cistern
         with mighty sliv[ered] short ))))))))))))))
shadows. [...Water refracts rays...]     [At a distance...the sea is dead.]
To ] repair                         (the)
(                                                               )
((                                                             ))
(((                                                           )))
moon [plant her] ((  [...]           as (Pistacia lentiscus) in     ))))
(((((                                                       )))))
((((((                    [limestone] until she       () blooms ()  ))))))
(((((((                                                    )))))))
((((((((               [Scrape stalks / chew {{ yellow }} resin]  ))))))))
((((((((((                                               ))))))))))
(((((((((((( [...Taste with]             (((((lunar))))) ))))))))))))
(((((((((((((                                          )))))))))))))
((((((((((((((((((.)   tongues [...] forever.... (*))))))))))))))))))))
```

| Poems to God |

Can't this singing

which all beings bring
be nothing less than
bird song or
poem

or riddling rhyme? I
don't need a grand
hymn sung as
though

infinite time were
spinning her
apocalyptic
wonders.

Can't this singing be
one brief note that
catches my heart
as in some
net

and flings it back to God?

Elizabeth Pinborough

Psalm of the Everyday Woman

1. Let me come to Your good garden, Lord,
   open Ye her gates. Nurture me there, Lord,
   my soul is cast down.
2. Till in my heart, Lord, rows of good earth,
   brim with seeds and watered with Thy grace.
3. You are the Gardner, Lord, keep Thou my feet,
   planted in rows, rooted in grace.
4. I am Your plant, Lord.
5. Grow me good and strong. Give me pure light, Lord,
   and nourish my roots.
6. You are the Water, Bread, and Life; Light and Truth,
   Foot-lamp and Sword. Pure is Your Word.
7. Pure is Your light. Purest waters running down.
8. You Are Honeycombe-Drinker, Bee-Fashioner,
9. Heart's Cartographer, Compass-Center,
10. Physician of Mercy, Sure Midwife,
11. Soul's Arborist, Brother & Friend,
12. Caritas. He of the Broken Wing.
13. Cast Your Piercing Eye into the vale of my life, Lord.
14. Please, נָא,
15. Map the Way out of mayhem.

Of course

Instead of 10,000
you gave me one

round

to hold—my own
head

hung

in my tiny
trembling hands

balancing

ball of bone
against

palms

against uncertainties
of healing.

Elizabeth Pinborough

Within

that rock
a fabulous

flint

of mind
still worked,

singing

the hymn,
of course

God

*speaks though
stones.*

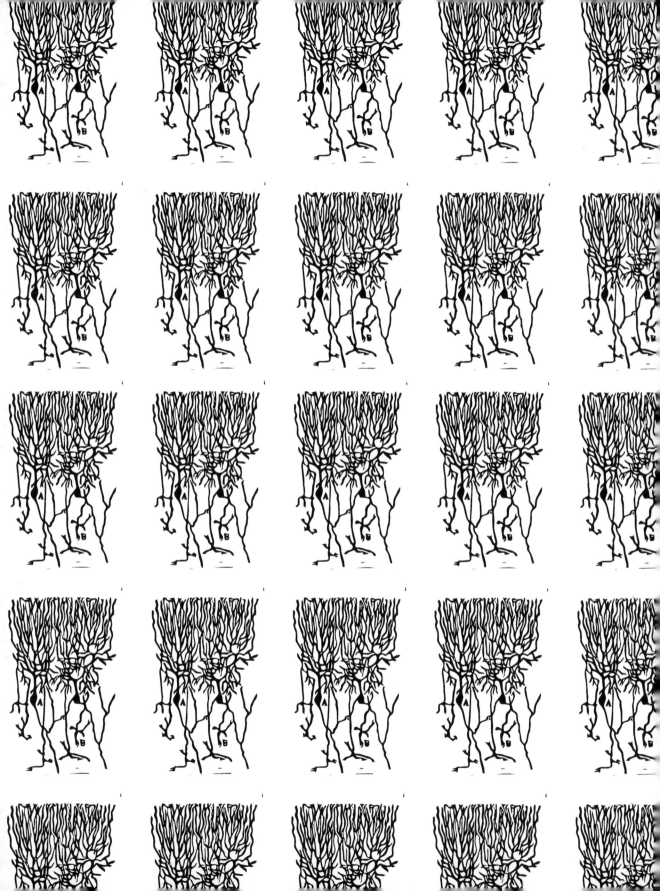

out from the company of bees
Psalm 118:5, 12

The wisdom of my mind's
escape is not mine, Lord.

Bees, wing and stinger,
dive with swarming

swords and bucklers.
Their eyes slit a

golden fury.

When

will You,

Lord, set me in a
large place: forsythia,

stem and bush, floral arms
to {brace} cruel companions?

The altar thickens with Your
honey, Lord, my keen salvation.

Elizabeth Pinborough

Threshing with God: A Psalm of Brain Injury

For months you felt mute, or rather, I did.

Words that would pearl from my tongue to your ear would not come.

I drifted in quarter consciousness like a raft on the sea—much deeper, more fathomless, than I knew it could be. For I was a sure swimmer in linguistic streams who could speak before, before she could walk.

What a cruel baptism in a black wordless realm for a yelping whelp of a tiny girl once grown wild and now grown small again.

When all I could do was sit in a stupor, beside my bed, head dumb with ache, brain thrashed, confused, undone,

you gave me a dream.

I am in a forest at night with one bright star. I walk toward the star and find I'm on a hill in a clearing wide.

Hello, Polaris, dear Christ star, who never wanders, who never fades. Hello, hope! Hello, way.

What was the hope? What was the way? Where was the path through the forest day after unfathomable day?

Elizabeth Pinborough

Who threshed the path on that moonbright hill? Who planted the trees? Who placed the star? Who found me?

Then, I remember another dream. Joseph Smith, that misapprehended visionary man, that frontier believer who tested God's word tensile and found it made of light, steel, sacrifice, and blood.

In his dream, he was swimming in very deep waters, and looking below he saw a school of great fish.

I've always believed this was a kind of sea of his mind, of going far beyond the capacity of a very capable swimmer, of glimpsing God's aquamarine fathoms.

The mind is our joy and our prison, our raft and our sea. But One undergirds it all.

Our captain, our friend. He.

God of leaving and return

God of leaving and return,
God of sight and sense,
God of passage and occlusions,
God of bright and bent,
Hear us pray.

Hear us when our hearts beat prayers for those we love.
Hear our cursing at the firmament.
Hear our twisted tongues mumbling bruised rhymes.
Hear us when we riddle and reason and cry.

And not.

You have mansions, Lord,
in your economy,
for the least of these—
Mansions of verse,
when walls won't do.

God of leaving and return:
You have metaphors to fill the universe.

Repent and come to our aid.

Elizabeth Pinborough

Wailing Psalm

1. I wail to You, O God.
2. I whisper prayers through cracks in rocks;
3. My brain petitions You as my voice surrenders speech.
4. My body's temple crumbles, Lord. Can You not see?
5. Many are cryptless now, God.
6. Like Yours, their tombs are borrowed from the earth.
7. Zion descends too slowly. Her jeweled foundations fade.
8. Light dims; resurrection's doomed, it seems.
9. In this uneasy dream, I cry above the foam.
10. Your Spirit broods over these waters, *tohu wa-bohu*.
11. Still, I wail to You, O God.

Elizabeth Pinborough

Crux

Blue lord,
    You are
        tangled in
            threnody—
    at the apex.
    Stars bead
the altar,
    appear
        circumpolar
            to southern
        believers.
    Scarlet god,
Your lights
    are five scars
        afire with
            five ways
        of knowing.
    You God
wear a
    surplice
        sewn of
            Coalsack,
        an ephod
    fit with
onyx

Elizabeth Pinborough

couched
in gold.
Your pierced
flesh—
needle
through
which my eye
must pass—
shows Self
emptying
Self.
Each peacock
feather of
Your crown
shapes a portal,
jewels fitting
my pilgrim's
path.
True Indigo,
Flower crushed
to dye, Plant
mashed to powder,
color my
salvation.

January 21, 2019

Hello, God, small and obscure, distant twinkly point of light.
Perhaps, you are the portal and I am the time. I long
thought the other way 'round.

I whistle through this little quiet
corridor of space, an earthly continuum—

waiting.

Waiting for the advance.
Waiting for the Final Anointing.
Waiting to be called up.
Waiting to be chosen.

The giant night pearl blisters red, shrouded by earth-shadow.

I, your little girl with a willing heart, am ashes,
burned to the ground of being, which is to say—
whatever spiritual geometry you find, whatever
compass and square with which you shape my mind,
whatever plumb line you drop into eternity's pool,

whatever thread with which you spool and unspool my nerves—
come back, O God! Come back to me.

Elizabeth Pinborough

Do not hide yourself in lunar umbra. Reveal the light of your
   shining.
From behind the sun's weak glare, release your radiance.
   Consume
my heart with your lively burning. Infuse my cells with every
   wavelength
of love you possess.

Notes

Epigraph 1 "Wall Piece for Orchestra to Yoko Ono," in *Grapefruit: A Book of Instruction and Drawings by Yoko Ono* (New York: Simon & Schuster, 2000), no page number.

Epigraph 2 Joseph Smith, Letter from Liberty Jail (1839), author transcription from the original held in the Church History Library, Salt Lake City, Utah.

The Brain's Lectionary The Hebrew word *nephesh* (נֶפֶשׁ) is translated as body, life, mind, seat of emotions and passions, and soul (see Strong's H5315).

Pseudoliparis swirei out of water are not very lovely to look at—like an uncooked chicken tender. Submerged in their habitat, the Mariana Trench, they appear ethereal, ghostly. Caught in 2014, *Pseudoliparis swirei* are the deepest species of fish documented, with one being filmed at a depth of 8,178 meters (see "Deepest Fish Ever Recorded—Documented at Depths of 8,178 m in Mariana Trench," press release by Japan Agency for Marine-Earth Science and Technology, August 24, 2017, https://www.jamstec.go.jp/e/about/press_release/20170824/. Accessed November 24, 2020).

Grief visits again (*swim, girl, swim*)   Gertrude Ederle was the first woman to swim across the English Channel. Her historic swim, from France to England, was documented in the short film *Swim, Girl, Swim.* Journalist Alec Rutheford described Ederle as a "pretty tiny atom of humanity" (See Gavin Mortimer, *The Great Swim* [New York: Walker & Company], 137. The inspiration for this poem was Adrienne Rich's "Diving into the Wreck," in Gelpi, Albert, Barbara Charlesworth Gelpi, and Brett C. Millier, eds., *Adrienne Rich Selected Poems: 1950–2012* (New York: W. W. Norton, 2018) 120–23.

Dorcas Resurrexit   I wrote this a few years before my injury, but it was published during my recovery. Both Dorcas and Peter can be dual types within the archetype of the wounded healer.

Ekphrasis on a sagittal brain slice by Drs. Greg Dunn & Brain Edwards   *Self Reflected* took two years of artistic and neuroscientific endeavor. To create an animated image of brain circuits communicating, Drs. Greg Dunn and Brian Edwards used "a combination of hand drawing, adapted neuroscientific data, algorithmic simulation of neural circuitry, photolithography, strategic lighting design, and gilding." By hand, they coated twenty-five microetched plates with 1,750 sheets of 22K gold leaf. The Franklin Institute in Philadelphia displays the original, which stands 8' × 12' tall and shows a 22x scale representation of the brain. Through reflected light, 500,000 neurons animate, and the viewer experiences what the brain looks like in action for 500 microseconds (see "How *Self Reflected* Was Made," http://www.gregadunn.com/self-reflected/how-self-reflected-was-made. Read a full description of their process there.).

Purkinje ekphrasis   Dr. Dana Simmons graduated from the University of Chicago with a PhD in neurobiology. Her research sought to understand how autism affects the cells of the cerebellum, where Purkinje cells are prevalent. Inspired by Andy Warhol and his art of the everyday object, Dr. Simmons brought art and science together to create psychedelic portraits of individual Purkinje cells, which have a unique pattern and structure visible throughout nature. Watch her book talk "Trees Inside Your Brain: Exploring the Purkinje Pattern" delivered to New England BioLabs, YouTube, December 21, 2016, which is the inspiration for this poem. https://youtu.be/HP88ZDznxhU.

Klaus, the Diatomist, navigates by light of phytoplankton Diatom arrangement came into fashion during the Victorian era. Klaus Kemp is a British man who has revived this art. He is featured in a short documentary film by Matthew Killip, called *The Diatomist* on Vimeo.

A guide to healing is inspired by the zen koan "A Scholar Writes a Treatise" in Kirchner, Thomas Yuho, trans., *Entangling Vines: A Classic Collection of Zen Koans* (Somerville, MA: Wisdom Publications), 61–62. The plant is *ocimum sanctum*. The goddess is Lakshmi.

A Psalm for - - - - - - - The title is borrowed from Shakespeare: "Shall quips and sentences and these paper bullets of the brain awe a man from the career of his humour?" (Shakespeare, *Much Ado About Nothing*, II.iii.240–42). This poem was inspired by Layli Long Soldier's "We," in *Whereas: Poems* (Minneapolis, MN: Graywolf Press, 2017), 47.

Psalm of the Everyday Woman נָא is a "particle of entreaty or exhortation, I (we) pray, now (enclitic)," "used by one craving a favourable hearing" (Brown, Francis, S. R. Driver, and Charles A. Briggs, *The Brown-Driver-Briggs Hebrew and English Lexicon* [Peabody, MA: Hendrickson Publishers, 2010], 609) (see Strong's 4994).

Threshing with God: A Psalm of Brain Injury The dream I am referring to is recorded in Joseph Smith's journal as follows: "Dream.— last night dreamed of swimming in a river of pure water clear as crystal, over a school of fish. of the largest <size> I ever saw. they were directly under my belly— I was astonished & felt afraid they might drown me or do me injury. they were the largest I ever saw.—" (Joseph Smith, Journal, March 15, 1843, p. 10, in Hedges, Andrew H., Alex D. Smith, and Richard Lloyd Anderson, eds. *Journals, Volume 2: December 1841–April 1843* [Salt Lake City: Church Historian's Press], 2011). For a long time, my healing journey felt like a constant struggle not to drown with none of my usual life-saving devices, including God. I love the idea of a spiritual reality being so vast and ocean-like that it includes many states, including the hazardous, the unfamiliar, and the mundane.

January 21, 2019 was the date of the total lunar eclipse I observed in Salt Lake City, Utah. I wrote the poem the same night. The moon was a super blood wolf moon.

Wailing Psalm *Tohu wa-bohu* (תֹהוּ וָבֹהוּ) is translated as formlessness and emptiness (see Strong's 8414 and 922). Empty emptiness.

Images

A cyanotype of "Cystoseira granulata" from Anna Atkins, *Photographs of British Algae: Cyanotype Impressions*, in Spencer Collection, The New York Public Library. New York Public Library Digital Collections. Accessed August 3, 2020, public domain. http://digitalcollections.nypl.org/items/510d47d9-4b3f-a3d9-e040-e00a18064a99. (Page 44.)

A cyanotype of "Chondrus crispus" from Anna Atkins, *Photographs of British Algae: Cyanotype Impressions*, in Spencer Collection, The New York Public Library. "Chondrus crispus" New York Public Library Digital Collections. Accessed August 3, 2020, public domain. http://digitalcollections.nypl.org/items/510d47d9-4b2a-a3d9-e040-e00a18064a99. (Page 43.)

A cyanotype of "Fucus canaliculatus" from Anna Atkins, *Photographs of British Algae: Cyanotype Impressions*, in Spencer

Collection, The New York Public Library. "Fucus canaliculatus" New York Public Library Digital Collections. Accessed August 3, 2020, public domain. http://digitalcollections.nypl.org/items/ 510d47d9-4b4c-a3d9-e040-e00a18064a99. (Pages 80–81.)

A bowl of bright apples   original illustration. (Page 38.)

Bison on Antelope Island   original illustration. (Page 32.)

Delineation of basal ganglia and basal forebrain neuroanatomy   Edlow, B.L., Mareyam, A., Horn, A. et al. "7 Tesla MRI of the *ex vivo* human brain at 100 micron resolution." *Sci Data* 6, 244 (2019).   https://doi.org/10.1038/s41597-019-0254-8.   Creative Commons BY 4.0 (http://creativecommons.org/licenses/by/4.0/).

To create my rendering, I traced a printout of the original images (front, inset) by hand, deciding which lines would create the best artistic representation. I have not intentionally altered anything and have done my best to maintain fidelity to the original. I am grateful to the 58-year-old woman who allowed her brain to be imaged for scientific and medical advancements, and I honor her life and unique neuroanatomy. The brain is still a vast unmapped country, and every image of every brain moves us collectively closer to understanding and healing its mysterious workings when wounded. (Pages 6–7, 25, 60, 99, endpapers.)

Diatoms (50 Species)   Randolph Femmer, USGS. Taken in the U.S. on Tuesday, March 15, 2016. Accessed August 3, 2020, public domain. https://www.usgs.gov/media/images/diatoms-50-species-3. (Page 84.)

Diatoms (Multiple Species)   Randolph Femmer, USGS. Taken on Sunday, January 1, 2006. Accessed June 2, 2021, public domain. https://www.usgs.gov/media/images/diatoms-multiple-species. (Page 62.)

Drawing of Purkinje cells (A) and granule cells (B) from pigeon cerebellum by Santiago Ramón y Cajal, 1899. Instituto Cajal, Madrid, Spain, public domain. (Pages 75, 124–125.)

Flower with bee   original illustration. (Page 127.)

Light, more light   original illustration. (Page 131.)

Mortar and pestle   original illustration. (Page 133.)

Mount Olympus at night, with walnut tree   original illustration, the view from my front yard. (Page 13.)

Pharmacy jar   early 1400s, Italian, on view at The Met Fifth Avenue in Gallery 307, public domain. (Page 103.)

Pomegranate   original illustration. (Page 31.)

Praying hands   original illustration. (Page 97.)

The pyramidal neuron of the cerebral cortex   Santiago Ramón y Cajal, 1904, ink and pencil on paper. Instituto Cajal, Madrid, Spain, public domain. (Pages 22–23, 104.)

The things they carried   illustration based on Assyrian relief in the British Museum. See images 7 and 8 in Sarah Lasarus, "Rare 3,000-year-old sculpture sells for \$31M, smashing record for Assyrian art," CNN, October 29, 2018. https://www.cnn.com/style/article/assyrian-relief-panel/index.html. Accessed November 24, 2020. (Page 116.)

X-ray of my skeleton   original illustration. (Page 110.)

Untimely figs   original illustration. (Pages 90–91.)

Publications

Thank you to the editors of the following publications who published these works.

"Crux," forthcoming in *Windows of Agates*.

"January 21, 2019," in *Dialogue: A Journal of Mormon Thought* vol. 52, no. 1 (Spring 2019), 87.

"Photo 51," in *Exponent II*, vol. 39, no. 1 (Summer 2019), 15.

"Immediately, a Poem," Segullah.org, October 8, 2018.

"Psalm of the Everyday Woman," Segullah.org, July 9, 2018.

"Threshing with God: A Psalm of Brain Injury," Mormon Women Project, June 14, 2018.

"*Perhaps* bisects my lamentation": An early version of this appeared as a prose poem in "Angels at My Side: Two Stories," Segullah.org, April 14, 2018.

"Dorcas Resurrexit," *Exponent II*, January 2016, 36–39.

Thank you, friends

To my mom, Jan Pinborough, my first and best editor, writing mentor, and friend, I give great thanks for help in crafting this book.

I owe the unfolding resurrection of my literary self to Kathryn Knight Sonntag, dweller in mountain forests of the feminine divine, and Alirezah Tagdarreh, the Persian transcendentalist, whose faith in me exceeds my own and who offers continual literary fellowship from Tehran.

Thank you to my co-editor and friend Sarah Page Parent for her enduring patience as I struggled to read poems and respond to our deadlines. For my friend Betsy VanDenBerghe, constant supporter and believer, much gratitude.

For Megan Goates and Jennie LaFortune, thank you for kindly tending to me in my woundedness and feeding me with your gorgeous words.

For the women of Sugarhouse Poetry Collective, Melody Newey Johnson, Twila Newey, Terresa Wellborn, Dalene Rex Rowley, and Linda Hoffman Kimball for your kind feedback and helpful edits. For all kind friends who have cheered me on in my recovery. Thank you!

Thank you to my dear friends and literary mentors who reviewed this book: Kimberly Johnson, Dayna Kidd Patterson, and Steven Peck.

My dream to publish a book with my illustrations felt as though it died with my injury. I am especially grateful to Michael Austin for accepting this manuscript and to Andrew Heiss for typesetting the intricate shape poems beautifully and for designing a truly artful table of contents. I have drawn courage from the beautiful work BCC Press is releasing by and for women, and by women who have experienced some of the extremes of the human experience and have brought forth creative diamonds. I am honored and grateful for my work to join this group of women and men who are offering their literary works as healing balms to a world weary from too much suffering.

Thank you, friends

Elizabeth Pinborough is an author, artist, and brain injury survivor who lives in Salt Lake City. She is an avid student of human development and neuroscience and delights in exploring the intersections of faith, science, and art. Her prayer journal, *Kindly Light Prayer Journal*, helps people develop a gentle relationship with daily prayer and is available on Amazon. Her poetry appears in *Dove Song: Heavenly Mother in Mormon Poetry*, *Dialogue: A Journal of Mormon Thought*, *Exponent II*, and *Fire in the Pasture: 21st Century Mormon Poets*. She edited the book *Habits of Being: Mormon Women's Material Culture*, published by Exponent II. She co-edits the literary and arts journal *Young Ravens Literary Review*. Visit her website at www.elizabethpinborough.com and follow her on Instagram @elizabethpinborough and Twitter @epinborough.

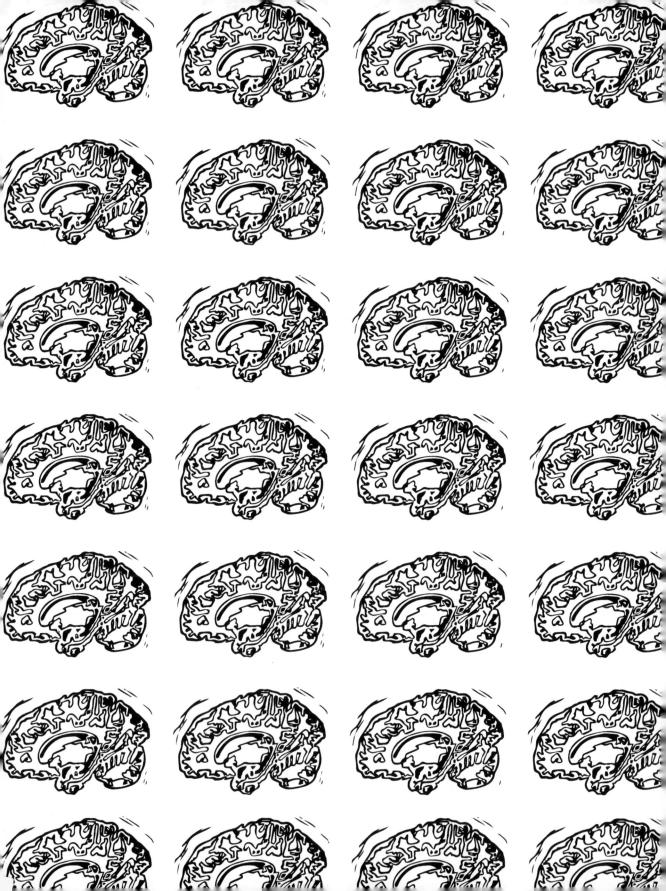

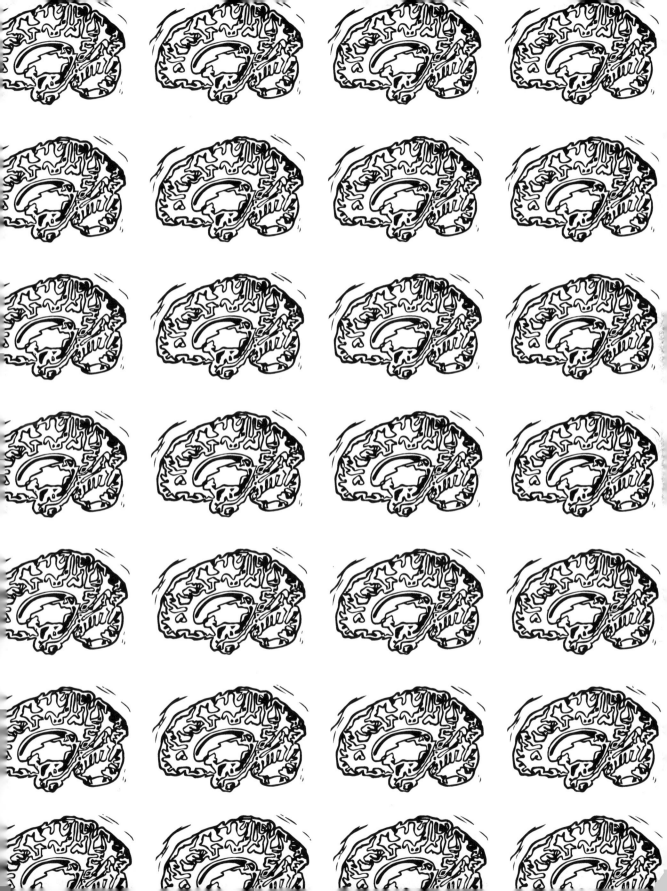